Convers

Imperial	Metric
1 pint (pt.)	568 ml
1 pound (lb.)	454g
1 ounce (oz.)	28g
Tablespoon (tbsp.)	15 ml
Teaspoon (tsp.)	5 ml
Cup = 8 oz	250 ml
Stick = 4 oz	125 ml

***

Oven temperatures

°C	°F	Gas Mark	Description
110	225	¼	Cool
120/130	250	½	Cool
140	275	1	Very Low
150	300	2	Very Low
160/170	325	3	Low to Moderate
180	350	4	Moderate
190	375	5	Moderately Hot
200	400	6	Hot
220	425	7	Hot
230	450	8	Hot
240	475	9	Very Hot

Cooking is about taste, not accurate measurement

Menu

Pâté & Soup	3
Beef & Venison	9
Chicken	15
Fish & Prawns	21
Lamb	24
Pork	27
Pasta	34
Flans	38
Vegetables	41
Puddings	45
Cakes & Snacks	50
Index	60

Pâté & Soup

Cheese and Herb Pâté *Serves 10 - Freezes*

450g good cream cheese
150g butter
3 garlic cloves crushed with a little salt

1 tbsp. fresh chervil, chopped
1 tbsp. parsley, chopped
1 tbsp. chives, chopped

- Mix the other ingredients evenly together, when the melted butter has cooled put it gently into the cream cheese, folding in very carefully.
- Leave to cool and set, either in a bowl or a loaf tin.

Chicken Liver Pâté *Serves 2 - Freezes*

110g chicken liver
1 slice green bacon
1 slice onion
1 small garlic clove, crushed

1 tbsp. beef gravy
1 tbsp. brandy
Butter

- Remove rind but leave fat on bacon
- Finely chop all of the ingredients
- Fry in a little butter until the onion has gone a gentle brown and the red has gone from the liver
- Liquidise adding gravy, enough to make it semi-liquid
- Add brandy and liquidise again
- Pour into ramekin or similar container
- Separately clarify some butter and pour over the top to seal
- Leave in the fridge to cool and chill.

Smoked Trout Pâté *Serves 2 - Freezes*

1 pack of 2 smoked trout fillets with dill
Butter – use an amount equal to half the weight of the trout

2 tbsp. double cream
1 tbsp. horseradish sauce
2 tbsp. lemon juice
Salt and pepper to taste

- Using softened butter, mash the trout into it then add the other ingredients, using more to taste as required.
- Chill
- Decorate with a little chopped parsley before serving.

Turkey or Pheasant Pâté *Serves 2 - Freezes*

225g minced/chopped cooked turkey or pheasant
150g butter
1 tsp. sherry

½ tsp. lemon juice
Pinch ground cloves
Salt and pepper to taste
2-3 drops Tabasco sauce

- Cream 100g butter and mix with the meat
- Add sherry, lemon juice, cloves and Tabasco sauce
- Stir well
- Salt and pepper to taste
- Pot up and smooth surfaces
- Melt remaining butter and pour over to cover surfaces
- Cover with foil and chill.

Curried Parsnip Soup *Serves 6 - Freezes*

50g butter
2 onions, diced
3 stick of celery, sliced
2 tbsp. mild curry powder
1 clove garlic, crushed or chopped

1 tbsp. flour
1.6 l vegetable stock
500g parsnips, chopped
Single cream

- Melt the butter and cook the onions and celery with curry powder until they are soft
- Add the garlic for the last minute
- Then add the flour and cook for another 2 minutes
- Pour in the stock and the chopped parsnips and cook until the parsnips are tender, usually about 20 minutes
- Allow to cool slightly and then blend with a hand blender or liquidise
- Reheat gently and add some cream before serving.

Fish Soup

6-8 shallots, finely chopped
½ bottle white wine
Fish stock
Tarragon
Ground black pepper
Chopped Parsley
Approx. 450g mixture of raw prawns, squid, mussels, fish pieces
140ml single cream
140ml crème fraîche
Olive oil
A tsp. of cornflour can be used to thicken if desired
For this recipe the amounts of each ingredient are not critical.

- Gently fry but do not brown, shallots in a little olive oil
- Add wine, tarragon, fish stock and ground black pepper
- Bring to a gentle simmer and then add chopped parsley, mussels, squid and fish
- Add cream and half of the crème fraîche
- Simmer for 15-20 minutes, add prawns for last five minutes
- Season to taste, add cornflour to thicken if desired
- Add remaining crème fraîche and a little parsley for decoration.

French Onion Soup *Serves 6 - Freezes*

350g onions, finely sliced
40g butter
900 ml beef stock
Freshly ground black pepper to taste

1 tbsp. dry sherry (optional)
4 slices French bread
50g grated cheddar cheese

- Fry onions gently in butter in a saucepan until soft and golden in colour
- Pour in stock, season to taste and bring to the boil
- Cover the pan and simmer for 45 minutes
- Add sherry
- Grill the bread with cheese on top and float on the soup to serve.

Roasted Red Pepper Soup *Serves 4 - Freezes*

4 red peppers, halved and deseeded
1 tbsp. oil
1 onion finely chopped
3 garlic cloves, sliced

1 tbsp. tomato purée
500g Stock
1 tin chopped tomatoes
A few fresh basil leaves

- Preheat oven to 160°C
- Put peppers onto baking tray, drizzle with oil then roast for 20 minutes
- Fry onions at a low heat and then for last minute add Garlic
- Add tomato purée, warm through
- Let peppers cool, then take off skins and chop
- Add peppers, tinned tomatoes and stock to onion mixture
- Bring to the boil and then simmer for 5 minutes
- Season to taste and then put into blender
- Serve with a garnish of basil leaves.

Roasted Red Pepper, Sweet Potato & Onion Soup
Serves 6-8   Freezes

2 red peppers, halved and deseeded
2 onions, peeled and quartered
1 large sweet potato, peeled and chopped

2 tbsp. olive oil
900ml stock

- Preheat oven to 200°C
- Place all vegetables in a large roasting tin and toss in the olive oil
- Roast for approximately 30-40 minutes until soft
- When cooked, transfer to a large saucepan, cover with stock and simmer for 5 minutes
- Take off the heat and blend.

Tomato and Orange Soup *Serves 4 - Freezes*

1 medium onion, finely chopped
50g butter
2 level tbsp. flour
1 tin tomato juice
1 tin tomatoes

600g orange juice
2 tsp. sugar
½ tsp. basil or thyme
Salt and black pepper

- Sauté the onion in the butter until soft but not coloured
- Stir in the flour and cook for one minute, add tomatoes, tomato juice, orange juice, sugar and basil or thyme
- Bring slowly to the boil, reduce the heat and simmer for about 5 minutes
- Put soup through a sieve or liquidiser and return to the pan
- Season to taste
- Can be served hot or cold.

If serving cold, chill for several hours and dilute slightly with milk or cream.

Beef & Venison

Beef Carbonnade *Serves 6 - Freezes*

675g chuck or braising steak, cut into cubes
3 tbsp. plain flour
4 tbsp. vegetable oil
2 large onions, thinly sliced
1-2 garlic cloves crushed
275 ml brown ale
275 ml beef stock
2 tbsp. tomato ketchup or

1 tbsp. tomato purée
pinch ground mace or nutmeg
1 bay leaf
2 tsp. brown sugar
1½ tsp. French mustard
3-4 carrots, cut into sticks
100 g button mushrooms
chopped parsley /or coriander to serve
salt and freshly ground pepper

- Preheat the oven to 160°C.
- Coat the meat with flour seasoned with salt and pepper, then fry with 3 tbsp. oil until well browned. Transfer to casserole.
- Fry the onions and garlic with remaining oil until lightly coloured then add remaining seasoned flour and cook for 1 minute.
- Gradually add brown ale and stock and bring to the boil.
- Add ketchup, mace, salt and pepper, bay leaf, sugar, vinegar and mustard and pour over the beef.
- Add carrots to the casserole, mix well.
- Cover tightly and cook in the oven for 1¼ hours.
- Taste and season to taste, add mushrooms return for another ½ hour.
- Discard bay leaf, sprinkle parsley and serve.

Beef in Guinness *Serves 4 - Freezes*

650g diced beef
1 can Guinness
1 bay leaf
2 sprigs of thyme
1 onion, chopped
1 stick celery, chopped
2 rashers smoked bacon, roughly chopped

½ clove garlic, sliced
2 tbsp. olive oil
1 tbsp. flour
1 tsp. mustard powder
1/3 tin chopped tomatoes

- Start the day before!
- Cover the beef, bay leaf and thyme in the Guinness and leave, covered, in the fridge overnight or at least from morning till cooking time
- When ready to cook, preheat the oven to 150°C
- Strain the meat but reserve the marinade
- Heat half the oil in a large ovenproof pan and fry the meat, a few pieces at a time, until it is browned all over. Remove to a separate dish
- Add the rest of the oil and fry onion, celery and bacon for 5 minutes, adding the garlic for 1 minute at the end
- Stir in the flour and mustard powder and cook for one minute, stirring
- Return the meat to the pan and pour in the marinade liquid and the chopped tomatoes
- Cover the pan (if the lid is loose fitting, seal it with a sheet of foil) and place in the oven for 2½ hours
- This is delicious served with baked potatoes and a green vegetable but can be improved further by saving until the following day and adding dumplings.
- You may find that you need to add extra liquid to the casserole so that they have enough to cook in – water is fine if you don't have any more Guinness handy.

Dumplings *makes about 12*

110g self-raising flour
55g suet
30g bacon, finely chopped

1 tsp. mixed herbs
Water to mix

- Mix the flour and suet together, then add the chopped bacon and mix in with herbs
- Add water a teaspoon at a time until the mixture holds together and you can form small balls the size of walnuts
- Place these on top of a simmering casserole for the last 20 minutes of cooking time, turning them after 10 minutes.

Goulash *Serves 4-6 - Freezes*

1kg chuck steak, cubed
2 large onions, chopped
1 clove garlic, sliced
1 red pepper, sliced and deseeded
250g tomatoes, chopped
3 tbsp. tomato purée
3 tbsp. sunflower oil

300ml beef stock
150ml soured cream
1 tbsp. paprika
½ tsp. mustard powder
2 tbsp. seasoned flour
Salt and pepper to taste

- Preheat the oven to 160°C
- Coat the meat in the flour and mustard powder, sauté using an ovenproof casserole, until sealed
- Remove meat to warm plate, fry onions until lightly browned then add garlic, fry for a further half minute
- Blend in the stock and tomato purée
- Add red pepper, tomatoes, paprika and season to taste, then return meat to pan
- Mix well, bring to the boil stirring constantly
- Put into the oven and cook for 1¼ hours
- At the point of serving stir in the soured cream and garnish with parsley.

Steak and Kidney Pie *Serves 2-4*

500g diced beef
150g diced kidney
1 onion, finely chopped
2 tbsp. flour
1 tsp. mustard powder
Later:
100 g mushrooms, roughly chopped
Short crust pastry made with 175g flour and 75g butter
This is a two-stage recipe:

1 beef stock cube
1 tbsp. Worcestershire sauce
1 tbsp. mushroom ketchup
Water

Day One
- Preheat oven to 150°C
- Place the meat and onion in a casserole dish, sprinkle over the flour, mustard powder and crumbled stock cube and mix so that the pieces of meat are coated.
- Mix Worcestershire sauce and mushroom ketchup with a cup of water and pour over the meat. Add a little more water as necessary to come halfway up the mixture; it should not be swimming in liquid.
- Cover the dish with foil and place in the oven for an hour and a half
- Remove from oven and cool
- At this stage the mixture can be divided and or frozen until required.

Day Two
- Make short crust pastry and roll out slightly larger than required to fit the pie dish
- Place steak and kidney mixture in a pie dish and stir the chopped mushrooms through it
- Place a pie funnel in the middle of the dish
- Cut a thin strip of pastry to lay along the wetted edge of the pie dish; wet this with a little water so that the main piece of pastry will stick down
- Cut a cross in the middle of the main piece of pastry so that the pie funnel can stick through it, press down the edges and knock them up with a knife
- If there is leftover pastry, decorate the top with some leaf shapes
- Allow to cool and rest in the fridge for half an hour
- Preheat oven to 200°C
- Place pie in oven for 20 minutes then reduce heat to 180°C for another 20 minutes.

Venison Casserole *Serves 4-6 - Freezes*

2 tbsp. olive oil
2 medium onions, peeled and finely chopped
3 garlic cloves peeled and crushed
900g haunch of venison, trimmed and cut into large cubes
600ml cheap port
Salt and black ground pepper
3 tbsp. redcurrant jelly

- Preheat oven to 150°C
- Heat the oil in a large, deep, lidded flameproof casserole, add the onions and garlic and cook until golden brown
- Add the cubed meat in batches and increase the temperature so that the cubes fry and seal rather than 'stew'
- Remove each batch to a plate while frying another
- When all the cubes are sealed, return to the casserole
- Add three-quarters of the port and some salt and pepper
- Stir well, cover with the lid and cook for 2 hours
- Remove from oven, cool thoroughly and then chill
- Keep in fridge for four days before cooking
- On day of serving heat oven to 180°C
- Add the redcurrant jelly and remaining port to the casserole, mix and cook for 1½ hours
- Season to your taste.

Warming Beef Stew *Serves 4-6 - Freezes*

1 kg diced beef
30g lard
400 ml beef stock (or glass red wine made up to 400 ml with beef stock)
2 onions, roughly chopped
2 sticks celery, sliced
2 carrots, sliced
1 turnip, diced
½ swede, diced
1 parsnip, diced
1 can oxtail soup
1 bay leaf
Bouquet garni (or 1 tsp. mixed herbs)
12 prunes
Salt and pepper to taste

- Preheat oven to 150°C
- Fry meat in a casserole or heavy cast iron pan, a few pieces at a time to brown and seal each piece, remove to warm plate
- Add a little more lard if necessary and fry onions and celery for 5 minutes
- Add the rest of the vegetables stirring occasionally for 3 or 4 minutes
- Return the meat and add oxtail soup and another can full of water, bay leaf and bouquet garnish
- Bring to the boil; turn the heat down to keep it at a simmer.
- Put in the prunes, stir and season to taste then cover with a lid and cook slowly for 2 hours.
- This seems to taste even better if you allow it to cool and then reheat a day or two later.
- Add dumplings in the final 20 minutes if you like (see Beef in Guinness for recipe).

Chicken

Chicken and Stilton Roulades *Serves 4*

4 chicken breasts, skinned and boned
90g butter, softened
125g Blue Stilton cheese, crumbled
8 rashers smoked back bacon with rind removed
1 tbsp. vegetable oil
2 tbsp. butter
1 glass red wine made up to 300ml with chicken stock,
Salt and freshly ground pepper
1 level tsp. arrowroot (or cornflour)
Watercress to garnish

- Whisk the cheese and butter to a smooth paste
- Beat out the chicken breasts between two sheets of damp greaseproof paper
- Spread the butter mixture evenly on one side of each breast
- Roll up the chicken breasts and wrap in bacon rashers. Secure with wooden cocktail sticks
- In a heavy-based pan, heat the oil and butter and brown chicken rolls well
- Pour in the red wine and stock, season, bring to the boil, cover and simmer gently for 35-40 minutes, turning occasionally.
- Remove the cocktail sticks, place the chicken in a serving dish and keep warm
- Blend the arrowroot with a little water until smooth; pour into the pan juices and heat, stirring, until thickened
- Season and spoon sauce over the chicken
- Garnish with watercress sprigs.

Chicken Broccoli *Serves 4*

4 chicken breasts, skinned
Enough broccoli florets to cover the bottom of a baking dish
2 tbsp. mayonnaise
1 tbsp. curry powder
1 tin condensed chicken or mushroom soup
½ tin water
1 small clove garlic, crushed
3 tbsp. grated Cheddar cheese

- Preheat oven to 180°C
- Lay broccoli at the bottom of a baking dish
- Place chicken breasts on top
- Mix mayonnaise, soup, water and curry powder, pour over chicken
- Sprinkle with grated cheese
- Bake for 1 hour until crispy on top and chicken cooked through.

Chinese Chicken Salad *Serves 6*

750g chicken breast, cooked, cubed and cooled
3 pkt Top Ramen Chinese noodles, chicken flavour
450g cabbage, chopped
1 head of broccoli, broken into small pieces
3 green onions
100ml sesame oil
100ml water
6 tbsp. rice vinegar
3 tbsp. sugar
50g toasted sliced almonds
2 tsp. roasted sesame seeds
seasoning to taste

- Mix together chicken, chicken flavour, sesame oil, water, vinegar, sugar and chill
- Mix together vegetables and chill
- Just before serving mix chicken and vegetables together with almonds, sesame seeds
- Break up raw noodles and mix in.

Chicken Couscous *Serves 2*

2 chicken breasts, diced
1 onion, roughly chopped
1 stick celery, sliced
½ large carrot, sliced
½ large parsnip, diced
½ red pepper, chopped
½ green pepper, chopped
1 tbsp. olive oil
1 tbsp. sultanas, soaked in the stock
450ml chicken stock
3 tsp. Ras el Hanout spice
200g couscous

- Fry chicken in 1 tablespoon of olive oil in a deep pan until sealed on all sides
- Add a teaspoon of the spice and then the onion, celery and carrot and cook for 5 minutes, stirring
- Add parsnip and another teaspoon of spice, cook for 2 minutes and then add the stock
- Cook for 10 minutes then add the peppers, sultanas and last teaspoon of spice and cook for another 10 minutes
- Pour 300ml boiling water over couscous in a bowl and cover for 5 minutes
- Stir 1 tablespoon of olive oil into couscous and loosen with a fork before serving. There will be a lot of liquid, but the couscous on the plate will soak this up.

Creamy Cider Chicken *Serves 6-8 - Freezes*

6/8 chicken portions
1 onion chopped
1 eating apple, cored and cut into wedges
1 tbsp. plain flour
225 ml dry cider

- Heat half oil in large pan
- Season chicken with salt and pepper and cook until browned on all sides
- Remove onto warm plate
- Drain excess fat, add remaining oil , fry onion until soft
- Add apple and cook for a further 2-3 minutes
- Stir in flour and cook for a minute
- Add cider and bring to the boil for a couple of minutes
- Add stock, thyme, bay leaf and chicken
- Bring to the boil then simmer for 20-25 minutes or until the chicken is thoroughly cooked
- Stir in cream just before serving.

Chicken in Cider *Serves 4-6 - Freezes*

1 chicken
225g tomatoes, skinned and sliced (or a small can of tomatoes)
2 medium onions, sliced
1 clove garlic, sliced
300ml cider
1 tbsp. flour
½ tsp. mustard powder
2 tbsp. tomato purée
Salt and pepper to taste

- Preheat the oven to 190°C
- Fry chicken on all sides until golden brown
- Place into casserole with tomatoes, onion and garlic
- Add cider and season, bring to the boil, cover
- Bake for 1½ hours until tender
- Sieve flour and mustard powder together
- Strain off liquid and blend in flour mixture and tomato purée
- Bring to the boil and simmer for about a minute stirring all the time
- Pour over the chicken
  Alternatively use chicken pieces, which would cook more quickly.

Chicken Mornay *Serves 4*

1 chicken, jointed or 4 chicken pieces
75g butter
50g flour

1 tsp. French mustard
50g cheddar cheese, grated
1 tbsp. crushed cornflakes

- Preheat oven to 190°C
- Place chicken pieces into ovenproof dish and dot with 25g butter
- Bake in the centre of the oven for 20 minutes
- Melt butter, adding flour, cooking and stirring well for 2-3 minutes
- Carefully add milk mixing into a thin paste
- Add mustard and 50g cheese and cook gently for 5 minutes
- Cover chicken with sauce
- Sprinkle remaining cheese and cornflakes over chicken and return to oven for a further 10 minutes until cooked

Devilled Chicken *Serves 4*

4 chicken breasts, skinned
1 medium onion, chopped
1 garlic clove, sliced
50g margarine
2 tsp. mustard powder
1 tsp. curry powder

- Preheat oven to 190°C
- Gently fry the onion until soft, a minute before removing from the heat add garlic.
- Score each of the chicken breasts several times
- Beat margarine until soft, add all other ingredients and mix well
- Spread mixture over the chicken pieces liberally and place in fridge to marinade for at least 30 minutes, but overnight would be better.
- Place in the centre of the oven for 40 minutes
- Baste every 15 minutes, adding tbsp. water to loosen where necessary.

Waterzooi Gantoise *Serves 4-6*

1 large chicken	1/1.5 well flavoured and strong chicken stock
2 onions	4 egg yolks
2 shallots	100ml cream
3 leeks	Juice ½-1 lemon
3 sticks celery	1tbsp chopped parsley
3 carrots	Salt and pepper to taste
4 parsley roots	
60g butter	

- Chop finely all of the vegetables and stew gently in a large saucepan with half of the butter for about 20 minutes. The parsley roots should be put in whole and allowed to stew as well, it is these that give the dish its very authentic taste
- Cut the chicken into eight pieces and place on top of the vegetables
- Pour in sufficient stock to cover. Bring to the boil, cover the pan, simmer very gently until the chicken is cooked
- Remove the chicken to a warm plate
- Beat egg yolks and cream together with the remainder of the butter. Very gently mash the parsley roots into the egg and cream mixture
- Beat a teaspoon of the hot soup into the egg and cream mixture and then carefully add all of it to the soup being very careful not to curdle the cream
- Season with salt, pepper and lemon juice
- Add chopped parsley and chicken pieces.
  Serve with boiled potatoes.

Fish & Prawns

German Herring Salad

200g mayonnaise
300g pickled large gherkins
300g pickled whole beetroots
300g pickled herring
1 onion

1 apple
2 medium-sized boiled potatoes
1 stick celery
Salt and pepper to taste
Optional sliced hard-boiled egg

- Dice quite finely the apple, onion, potatoes, beetroots, herring, celery and gherkins.
- Mix together with the mayonnaise and salt and pepper in a large bowl. (Garnish with sliced hard-boiled egg if desired)
- Cover and leave in fridge for 12 hours or more and serve with crunchy bread.

Steph's Salmon Parcel *Per Person*

1 salmon fillet, approximately 120g
70g of uncooked couscous
1 carrot, diced
2 tablespoons of peas
2 tablespoons of sweet corn
½ onion, diced
1 tsp. capers

½ clove of garlic, sliced
½ lemon
Salt and pepper
Sour cream
200ml in total of vegetable stock
and dry white wine

- Preheat oven to 180°C
- Tear off a generous sized piece of tin foil and butter
- Place the couscous, vegetables in the middle of the foil, put the salmon fillet on top
- Squeeze half a lemon over and season
- Add vegetable stock/ wine
- Close parcel up with a double fold at the top and the sides
- Cook for 20 minutes
- Carefully undo the foil, add dollop of sour cream, sliding the couscous, vegetables and salmon onto a pre-warmed plate and serve with the other half of the lemon.

Trout with Almonds and Dill *Per Person*

1 trout
1 tbsp. ground almonds
1 tbsp. sliced almonds

1 tsp. dried dill or more if fresh
Large knob of butter

- Use a flat-bottomed frying pan
- Cut the head off the trout, wash thoroughly and dry, then roll in the ground almonds. Sprinkle half the dill inside the trout
- Heat butter till it stops hissing
- Fry the trout for 4 minutes on one side without burning then fry for 5-6 minutes on the other side on a slightly lower heat
- Remove the fish to serving dish, fry the almonds for 1 minute
- Drain the almonds and sprinkle over the fish with the rest of the dill and a squeeze of lemon.

New Orleans Prawns *Serves 4*

50g butter
3 or 4 sticks celery, chopped
1 large onion, diced
1 clove garlic, sliced
1 green pepper, diced
500g jumbo prawns
1 tin condensed cream of mushroom soup

Water
350g rice, long grain
2 tbsp. parsley, chopped
Parsley, garnish
Ground black and cayenne pepper

- Melt the butter in a large pan and cook the celery for 10 minutes, without browning
- Put the rice on to cook and drain when cooked but meanwhile
- Add onion to the celery and continue cooking for 5 minutes
- Add diced pepper and garlic to the vegetables for 2 minutes
- Add soup to the vegetables plus half a tin of water
- Add prawns to the mixture and stir over a low heat; if it looks dry, add a little more water
- Add parsley and stir into the mixture
- Add the cooked rice to the mix and adjust the seasoning with black pepper and cayenne

Heat through for a couple of minutes and then serve with parsley to garnish.

Prawn Stir Fry *Serves 2*

2 blocks of medium egg noodles
225g pack jumbo prawns
300g pack stir fry mix of vegetables
½ red pepper, sliced
½ green pepper, sliced
Extra bean sprouts as required

1 tsp. sunflower oil
1 handful cashew nuts
2 tbsp. soy sauce
1 tbsp. Worcestershire sauce
3 tbsp. dry sherry
Toasted sesame oil

- Heat oil in a wok and fry the cashews quickly till they take on a little colour, put aside and keep warm
- Boil water in a pan and put the noodle blocks in to cook as per packet instructions
- Add all the vegetables to the hot wok and fry them for 2 minutes, stirring frequently
- Add prawns to the vegetables, stir in
- Add the soy sauce, Worcestershire sauce and sherry, keep stirring and allow it all to heat through for 2 minutes
- Drain the noodles, add a little sesame oil and toss the noodles in the serving dish
- Add a little sesame oil to the wok then transfer to serving dish.

A really quick meal when you are anxious to eat in a matter of minutes. Finely shredded vegetables of almost any kind can be used as alternatives to pre-packed and quantities adjusted to serve more people.

Lamb

Amanda's Slow Cooked Lamb *Serves 4*

2 kg shoulder of lamb
1 tsp. oil
6 onions, roughly chopped
Thyme

12 cloves garlic
Bottle red wine
Salt and pepper

- Preheat oven to 200°C
- Rub lamb with oil, salt and pepper
- Place in the oven for 30 minutes with onions
- Remove and drain off fat
- Add garlic and thyme
- Cover and reduce temperature to 130°C
- Cook for 4½ hours
- Bring wine to the boil then pour over lamb
- Cook for a further hour
- Remove lamb, cover and allow it to rest
- The liquid should be reduced over a high heat.

Exmoor Poachers Pot *Serves 4*

450g meat, diced
225g mixed pulses
½ clove garlic, sliced
1 leek, sliced
1 carrot, chopped
1 onion, sliced
1 red pepper, diced
1 green pepper, diced

568 ml stock
1 tbsp. oil
1 tbsp. flour
½ tsp. mustard powder
Salt and pepper to taste
Optional, 1 glass wine from his Lordship's wine cellar

By its very nature the meat can be anything from sausages to venison, the stock depends on the meat as does the wine or, if it is a strong meat port can be used. Similarly, the vegetables can be any that are available

- Pre-soak pulses, as per packet instructions, if using dried pulses
- Preheat the oven to 180°C
- Sieve the flour and mustard and use to coat the meat.
- Heat the oil in a casserole, sauté the meat until brown and sealed all over
- Add the vegetables and fry gently with the meat until soft; add the garlic for the last minute.
- Add stock, wine and pulses, season to taste
- Bring to the boil, then cover and put into the oven for around 30-40 minutes or until tender.
- Alternatively simmer on top of the stove.

Lamb Shanks *Serves 2*

2 lamb shanks
6 tbsp. olive oil
1 medium onion, thinly sliced
1 medium carrot, grated
1 celery stalk, chopped
1 tin chopped tomatoes
1 tbsp. tomato purée

1 clove garlic, crushed / sliced
150ml red wine
150ml beef stock
Flour mixed with ½ tsp. mustard powder
110g mushrooms, quartered
Parsley, chopped
Lemon peel, finely grated

- Heat the oil
- Coat the lamb shanks with the flour and mustard mixture and fry until well browned
- Remove and then fry the onion, carrot and celery slowly until soft but not brown
- Stir in tomatoes, tomato purée, wine, stock and garlic
- Bring to the boil, season to taste
- Add lamb shanks
- *Cover the pan tightly and simmer very gently for 1½ hours
- Add mushrooms
- *Cover pan and simmer for another 30 minutes
- Serve with parsley and lemon peel sprinkled over

*Alternatively put into an oven preheated to 150°C

Liver Bonne Femme *Serves 4*

50g butter
350g sliced lambs or calves liver
110g lean bacon, diced
2 onions, roughly chopped
110g button mushrooms, quartered
2 tbsp. flour
300ml stock
Mixed herbs
A few new potatoes or thick slices of old potato
Small carton of cream
Seasoning to taste

- Preheat oven to 160°C
- Melt the butter and brown the liver quickly on both sides
- Transfer to an ovenproof dish
- Cook bacon, onions and mushrooms for around 5 minutes until onions are lightly browned.
- Blend in the flour and cook for a minute then gradually add the stock, stirring all the time until the sauce is smooth and creamy
- Season well and then pour over the liver
- Add herbs and then lay sliced potatoes over the top
- Cover tightly and put into the oven for 45-50 minutes, adding the cream just before serving.

Pork

Ann's Liver Casserole *Serves 4*

2 large onions, peeled and thinly sliced
450g pig's liver
225g streaky bacon smoked or un-smoked
(smoked gives a more salty taste but equally nice)
850ml good beef stock thickened to taste with corn flour, alternatively use
4 Beef Oxo cubes in 850 ml water
Small can baked beans

- Pre heat the oven to 160 degrees
- Fry onions slowly in a small amount of oil until transparent and lightly coloured
- Put the onions in the base of a casserole with the baked beans
- Wash the liver under cold water and lay on top of the onions (do not pre-fry)
- Lay the rashers of bacon on top of liver (again do not pre-fry)
- Pour stock over the contents of the casserole
- Season with salt and pepper.
- Gently stir the contents to mix together slightly.
- Place the casserole in the middle of the oven and wait until it is heated through and gently bubbling. At that point remove from oven and again gently stir the contents to make sure none are stuck to the bottom. Replace casserole lid and leave for 1½ hours reducing the temperature if it is cooking too fiercely. It needs to be cooked very gently to produce the soft melt in the mouth texture that is wanted for the liver.
- At the end of this time the heat can be increased to 200 degrees and dumplings can be added to the casserole. (See Beef in Guinness.)

Brian's Honeyed Gammon

Gammon joint
Bouquet garni (rosemary, thyme, sage and 3-4 bay leaves)
German mustard
Honey

- Cover gammon in water, and bring to boil
- Rinse in cold water to remove salt. (if possible leave in cold water overnight)
- Drain, cover again with cold water and add bouquet garni
- Bring to boil and gently simmer for 30 minutes per pound weight
- Preheat oven to 170°C
- Remove skin from gammon and diamond score the remaining fat
- It may be necessary to skewer gammon to hold together, and also to prop up on edge
- Smear mustard into the cuts and then lightly coat with honey
- Bake in oven for 15 minutes, whatever the weight.

Elizabethan Pork *Serves 6-8*

1 kg chump steaks or loin chops, cut into 3cm. chunks
½ bottle red wine
2 medium onions thinly sliced
2 tbsp. plain flour
1 tsp. plain mace
1 tsp. medium curry powder
450ml chicken stock
100g dried apricots
100g raisins
100g dried stoned dates or pitted prunes.

- Preheat oven to 160°C
- Fry the pork over high heat until well browned, remove
- Add onions and cook over a medium heat until softened
- Sprinkle over flour and spices stirring for 1 minute
- Stir in wine and stock and bring to a simmer
- Stir in the meat and fruit
- Slow cook in the centre of the oven for 2 hours.

Hunters Pork Chops *Serves 4*

4 pork chops or chicken joints
15g flour
2 tbsp. oil
2 small onions, sliced
2 small carrots, sliced
50g mushrooms
1 medium can of condensed tomato or mushroom soup.
140ml cider or dry white wine
1 tablespoon chopped parsley for garnish
1 bouquet garni
Salt and pepper

- Preheat oven to 180°C
- Heat oil in pan and brown chops (or joints)
- Lightly fry vegetables
- Mix soup with cider
- Put vegetables in casserole dish, then put meat on top
- Pour liquid over, season and put in bouquet garni, cover firmly
- Cook for 1½ hours
- When cooked take out bouquet garni.

Leeks and Ham au gratin *Serves 4*

4 leeks
4 slices of ham
50g margarine
50g flour

450ml of milk
125g grated cheese
2 tbsp. breadcrumbs
1 teaspoon mustard powder

- Preheat the oven to 190°C
- Cook the leeks and drain very well, saving the stock
- Wrap each leek in a slice of ham and place into a well-greased ovenproof dish
- Sieve the flour and mustard powder together
- Melt the margarine and add the flour mixture to the margarine slowly, heat but do not burn for 2 minutes
- Add the milk to make the white sauce and add ¾ of the cheese, pour over the ham rolls
- Mix the remaining cheese and breadcrumbs and sprinkle over the surface
- Heat in the oven for 20-30 minutes

Alternatively substitute celery, cut into 10 cm lengths and cook; or chicory, wash and then cook without salt, then continue as above.

Paprika Pork *Serves 4*

2 tbsp. vegetable oil
500g diced pork
2 carrots, peeled and sliced
2 onions, peeled and chopped
1 green pepper
250g can of peeled tomatoes

150ml chicken stock
2 tsp. paprika
Salt and black pepper
2 tbsp. water
2 tsp. cornflour

- Heat the oil in a saucepan and fry the pork till browned
- Add the onions and carrots and fry for 3 minutes then add green pepper and fry an other minute
- Stir in paprika, tomatoes, stock, and black pepper and bring to the boil
- Cover and simmer for 1 hour
- Blend cornflour with water and add to the pork until the sauce thickens
- Serve with baked potatoes.
- If desired soured cream or yoghurt can be spooned on top before serving.

Pork and Ginger Casserole *Serves 4*

675g boneless lean pork, cubed
1 small onion, chopped
1 tsp. ground ginger, level
30g flour
10g mustard powder
30g sugar
400g can Italian tomatoes
170g button mushrooms

2 tbsp. vinegar
1 tbsp. soy sauce
1 bay leaf
2 cloves garlic, crushed
55g stem ginger, sliced
1 red pepper, seeded and sliced
Salt and pepper to taste

- Preheat oven to 140°C
- Coat pork with a mix of flour, ground ginger, salt, pepper and mustard powder
- Fry a few at a time until browned then transfer to casserole
- Add chopped onion
- Add canned tomatoes, mushrooms, sugar, vinegar, soy sauce, garlic and bay leaf
- Cover tightly and cook for 1½ hours until meat is tender
- Remove bay leaf, add red pepper and stem ginger, cook for a further 10 minutes.

Pork Parcels *Serves 4*

4 pork chops
2 onions, sliced
1 clove garlic, sliced
2 peppers, deseeded and sliced
100g mushrooms, quartered

Juice of ½ lemon
50g butter
½ tsp. mustard powder
2 tsp. honey
200m dry cider

- Preheat the oven to 180°C
- Cut 4 large squares of aluminium foil
- Put each pork chop into the centre of its own foil square
- Mix butter, honey and mustard powder, divide equally between each of the pork chops
- Divide the rest of the ingredients between each of the pork chops
- Make a double fold at the top of the parcel and double folds at each end.
- Cook for 40 minutes or until meat is cooked, open parcels about 10 minutes from the end.

Sam's Sausage Hotpot *Serves 4*

1 large onion, thinly sliced
1 large cooking apple, sliced
450g white cabbage, shredded
2 large carrots, sliced
12 thin pork sausages, chopped into halves

110g streaky bacon, cut into thin strips
30g flour
30g lard
330ml chicken stock

- Preheat oven to 190°C
- Heat lard in a large ovenproof casserole, brown the sausages for a few minutes and then add the bacon strips to brown to.
- Stir in the onion and carrots, cooking for three minutes then add the apple slices and stir through
- Sprinkle over the flour and pepper to taste and stir for 2 minutes
- Put the shredded cabbage on top of the other ingredients
- Pour the stock over and seal with a well-fitting lid
- Cook in the oven for 50 minutes, stirring halfway through this time.

Sausage Meat Plait with Baked Apple *Serves 4-6*

454g puff pastry
330g sausage meat
30g butter
1 onion, chopped
1 leek, chopped
1 clove garlic, chopped

1 egg, beaten
60g breadcrumbs
3 cooking apples
1 red pepper
6 plums
3 rashers bacon

- Preheat oven to 220°C
- Roll out puff pastry on a floured surface to a square at least 25cm x 25 cm x, cut both sides into diagonal strips, leaving a 8cm strip clear down the middle
- Lightly cook onion and leek in butter until soft, adding garlic for the last minute
- Mix sausage meat, most of the egg (leaving some for glazing), breadcrumbs and cooled, cooked vegetables together
- Shape sausage mixture to fit down the middle of the pastry and plait the side strips across it to cover; brush with the remaining egg
- Place in centre of oven for 15 minutes, then turn oven down to 180°C for a further 30 minutes

While this is cooking prepare accompaniment:
- Dice pepper, plums and bacon and mix together
- Core apples, place the mixture in the hole and cook in medium oven, 180°C for 30 minutes.

Savoury Sausage Roly Poly *Serves 4*

1 medium Bramley apple, peeled, cored and chopped
200g sausage meat
2 tbsp. chopped onion
2 tbsp. parsley
200g plain flour
½ tsp. salt
2 tsp. baking powder
100g shredded suet
Cold water
1 beaten egg

- Pre-heat oven to 200°C
- Add apple to sausage meat with onion and parsley and mix well
- Sieve flour with salt and baking powder
- Mix in suet lightly
- Stir in sufficient cold water to make a soft but not sticky dough
- Roll out on a well-floured board with a rectangle 25cm wide, about ½ cm thick.
- Spread sausage mixture over the dough leaving a 2 cm. border all round
- Damp border lightly
- Roll up the dough, like a Swiss roll
- Press the ends and the join to seal
- Line a 900g loaf tin with a long strip of greased greaseproof paper, with width of the base
- Place the roll in the tin, join downwards
- Make 3 or 4 slits in the top to allow steam to escape
- Bake for 20 minutes.
- Lift roll out of the tin onto a baking tray. Brush over with beaten egg
- Return to oven for further 20 minutes until golden brown.

Spicy Spare Rib Chops *Serves 2 - 4*

4 spare rib chops
2 tbsp. Demerara sugar
2 tbsp. tomato ketchup
2 tbsp. soy sauce
6 tbsp. vinegar

150ml stock
1 tsp. ground ginger
¼ tsp. pepper
1 tsp. dry mustard
1 clove garlic, crushed

- Preheat oven to 200 °C
- Combine all of the ingredients
- Pour over 4 spare rib chops
- Cook for 1½ hours turning chops occasionally.

Pasta

Carbonara Pasta with Bacon *Serves 2*

200g linguine
Olive oil for frying
1 small onion, peeled and diced
1 clove garlic, crushed
100g smoked back bacon cut up small

100g chestnut mushrooms sliced
Half glass white wine
100g mascarpone
100ml double cream
25g parmesan grated

- Cook pasta according to packet instructions
- Heat the olive oil in a pan, add the onion and garlic and cook for one minute then add the bacon and continue cooking for 5 minutes, toss in the mushrooms
- Turn up the heat, add the wine, bubble until reduced by about half, stirring all the time
- Then stir in the mascarpone, cream and parmesan
- Drain the cooked pasta and mix into the sauce
- Serve with extra parmesan scattered over the top.

Emma's Mozzarella Pasta *Serves 3-4*

225g penne pasta
400g tin drained whole plum tomatoes
2 tbsp. olive oil
150g mozzarella cheese, diced
100g fresh parmesan cheese, grated (or 50g dried)
2 tbsp. chopped basil
Seasoning to taste

- Preheat oven to 200°C
- Cook the pasta as per packet instructions till tender
- While it is cooking, heat oil in a wide pan and break down the tomatoes with a wooden spoon while heating gently
  Add the mozzarella and half the parmesan with basil and seasoning
  Bring to the boil and remove immediately from the heat or the cheese will get very stringy
- Drain the pasta and place in a greased ovenproof dish
- Pour the sauce over the pasta and mix in
- Sprinkle the rest of the parmesan over the surface and bake in the oven for 10 minutes
- Serve hot with a green salad.

Macaroni Cheese and Tuna *Serves 2*

1 tin of tuna, preferably in spring water
150g macaroni
100g cheddar cheese, grated
½ onion, diced
½ clove garlic, sliced

1 tbsp. flour
25g butter
250 ml milk
Paprika / cayenne
Salt and Pepper to taste

- Cook macaroni
- Fry onions until light brown, adding garlic for the last minute
- Add flour to the pan, stirring to absorb it all, cook gently for 2 minutes without burning
- Off the heat add the milk slowly to the mixture to produce thin paste, then return to the heat
- Add cheese, melt and bring gently to the boil
- Drain tuna and then flake into sauce, add drained macaroni and mix well
- Add paprika/cayenne pepper to taste.

Pasta with Parma Ham *Serves 3-4*

250g pasta shapes, farfalle or similar
25g butter
1 onion, finely chopped
125g mushrooms, sliced or halved depending on size
375g courgette, thinly sliced
70g Parma ham, torn into pieces
200ml tub crème fraîche
75g fresh parmesan cheese, grated
Ground black pepper

- Cook the pasta as per packet instructions until tender
- While this is cooking heat the butter in a large frying pan and fry the onion and courgette for 4 minutes, then add the mushrooms for a further 3 minutes, stirring from time to time
- Add the ham, crème fraîche, parmesan and ground pepper and stir to mix
- Drain the pasta and mix into the pan, heat through and serve garnished with basil leaves.

Pasta Surprise *Serves 3-4*

300g pasta spirals, farfalle or similar
200g left-over cooked ham, chicken, turkey or pork, diced
1 onion, chopped
1 red pepper, diced
1 green pepper, diced
100g button mushrooms, halved
50g butter
25g flour
1 tsp. mustard powder
225ml chicken stock
100ml milk

- Fry the mushrooms quickly in half the butter in a deep pan, remove and keep warm
- Add the remaining butter, fry the onions until soft and then stir in the flour and mustard powder, cooking for a minute or two.
- Add liquids slowly until the flour is absorbed and the sauce comes to the boil and thickens
- Add peppers and diced meat, adjust seasoning and heat through for at least 5 minutes.
- Serve with freshly cooked pasta.

Flans

Bacon and Tomato Quiche *Serves 8 - Freezes*

225g quantity of short crust pastry
2 eggs
3 tomatoes, peeled and chopped
75g bacon rashers, diced

75g cheddar cheese, grated
1 small tin evaporated milk
½ tsp. mustard powder
Ground black pepper

- Preheat oven to 200°C
- Make pastry and line a 23cm diameter flan dish, put in the fridge to chill
- Beat eggs together with bacon, add mustard powder, chopped tomatoes and cheese
- Mix all together and add evaporated milk and ground black pepper to taste
- Pour into the flan case and place in the oven for 30 minutes, until firm and brown
- Can be served hot or cold.

Cheesy Butternut Pasties *Serves 4 - Freezes*

Filling:
2 tsp. olive oil
1 small red onion, chopped
1 clove garlic
200g butternut squash, peeled and diced
Fresh ginger, grated
1 tsp. ground cumin

200ml hot vegetable stock
75g spinach, roughly chopped
50g cheddar cheese, diced
Pastry:
250g plain flour
125g butter
1 egg, to glaze

- Preheat oven to 180°C
- Heat oil in a frying pan, add onion and cook for 5 minutes until soft
- Add garlic and butternut squash, cook for 5 minutes until squash begins to brown
- Add stock and simmer gently for 20 minutes until squash is just soft
- Take off the heat, stir in spinach and leave to cool
- Make pastry and cut out 3 x 18cm diameter circles
- Spoon some of the mixture into the centre of each pastry circle and top with cheese
- Brush egg around the edge of the pastry, fold up and pinch the top together to make into pasties
- Brush all over with egg and bake for 15-20 minutes until golden.

Mushroom, Egg and Cheese Tartlets

Cheese pastry
150g plain flour
75g butter
50g cheddar cheese, grated
½ tsp. mustard powder
Pinch cayenne pepper
Also need a tiny tartlets tin and 6cm fluted pastry cutter

Mushroom filling
15g Porcini
100g fresh mushrooms, finely chopped
1 shallot finely chopped
25g butter
1 tsp. fresh parsley, chopped
1 clove garlic, crushed
1 tsp. lemon juice
Salt and black pepper to taste

- Preheat oven to 200°C
- To make dough, rub butter into flour
- Then add cheese, mustard, cayenne and a little water
- Rest in fridge for 15 minutes then roll out thinly
- Cut out rounds to fit a tartlets tin
- Prick with fork, bake on high shelf for 15 minutes.
- Soak Porcini for 20 minutes in a bowl of boiling water
- Heat butter in frying pan and when foaming add shallot and garlic and cook over low heat for about 10 minutes When ready drain dried mushrooms and squeeze out moisture
- Chop finely and add to frying pan along with fresh mushrooms
- Cook gently for around 20 minutes or until moisture has evaporated leaving thick spreadable mixture
- Add parsley
- Remove from heat and add lemon juice, salt and freshly milled black pepper
- Spoon mushroom mixture into tartlet shells

Optional extra: is to put a slice of hard-boiled egg on top with a blob of mayonnaise.

Onion Tart *Serves 8 Freezes*

225g flour
200g butter
225g onions, finely chopped
150ml double cream

3 egg yolks
100g bacon
Seasoning to taste

- Make short crust pastry from 225g flour and 100g butter and line a 23cm diameter flan dish; allow to rest in the fridge for 30 minutes
- Preheat oven to 200°C
- Cook the onions gently in remaining butter until very lightly coloured
- Mix the 3 egg yolks into the cream and then stir it into the onions.
- Pour sufficient mixture into the flan case to fill
- Cut the bacon into strips and scald in boiling water for about two minutes; drain well on kitchen paper
- Lay the bacon on top of the mixture
- Bake in a hot oven for about 25 minutes.

Vegetables

Braised Red Cabbage

1 whole red cabbage, shredded
1 cooking apple, roughly chopped
1 onion, finely chopped

Demerara sugar
Vinegar
Butter

- Heat a small amount of butter in a large saucepan and gently cook the diced onion for 5 minutes
- On a medium heat, add one third of the shredded cabbage, half the chopped apple, one tablespoon of sugar and one tablespoon of vinegar
- Repeat with the next third of the cabbage, remaining apple and another spoonful each of sugar and vinegar, finishing off with the remaining cabbage.
- Add a knob of butter, another spoonful each of sugar and vinegar and pour about 5 tbsp. of boiling water over the top.
- Cover the pan with the lid and bring to the boil, simmer gently, stirring just once or twice, for 60 minutes
- This will then be ready to serve but you have cooked enough for several meals, depending on the size of your cabbage, so it can be reheated on successive days and just gets better and better

Optional extra: some bacon rinds or chopped ham can be added but this complicates the keeping properties of this healthy side dish

Fried Rice

100g basmati rice
2 tbsp. oil
1 small onion, chopped
100g chopped vegetables (carrots, peas, peppers, spring onions etc.)
250ml water
1tsp cumin and caraway seeds for flavour
Salt and pepper to season
2 green chillies, chopped (optional)

- Fry onions for several minutes
- Add cumin, caraway seeds, vegetables, chillies and continue frying
- Add washed and drained rice, stir for two minutes
- Pour in water and bring to the boil
- Cover the pan and cook on a very low heat for 10-15 minutes until water is absorbed and rice cooked.

Leeks in Red Wine

3 leeks, cleaned and sliced
25g butter
1 tbsp. olive oil

140ml red wine
140ml vegetable stock

- Fry the leeks in butter and oil till golden
- Add red wine and stock and cook, covered, for 5 minutes.

Mushrooms Polonaise

1 onion, finely chopped
450g mixed mushrooms (skinned if picked wild)
25g butter
150ml soured cream
Salt and freshly ground black pepper
Fresh parsley

- Wipe and then cut the mushrooms into even-sized pieces
- Melt butter in a large pan and fry the onion till golden then add the mushrooms and cook for 4-5 minutes. If they make a lot of juice, boil it off
- Stir in the soured cream, heat gently and season to taste
- Transfer immediately to warmed serving dish and sprinkle with chopped parsley.

Risotto *Serves 4*

225g basmati rice
1 onion, diced
1 stalk celery, chopped
1 clove garlic, sliced
50g butter

25g parmesan cheese
50ml white wine
550ml chicken stock
Parsley to garnish

Other Vegetables or cooked meats can be added to taste

- Melt 25g butter in frying pan, fry celery for a few minutes, then add onion and finally garlic
- Add rice and fry gently but not burning for two minutes
- Add white wine and mix
- Stir frequently, add small amount of stock every time that the liquid has been absorbed, this should take around 30 minutes
- Before serving add butter and parmesan stirring until mixed and serve with garnish of parsley.

If other vegetables or cooked meats are to be added, put these in after around 15 minutes so that they get thoroughly heated.

Rolled Mushroom Omelette

6 large eggs
100g mushrooms, sliced
2 red onions, cut into small wedges
100g low fat cream cheese

50g grated cheddar cheese
3 tbsp. oil
A little milk
Salt and pepper

- Preheat oven to 180°C
- Drizzle onions with oil and grill until brown, keep warm
- Whisk together eggs, milk, salt and pepper
- Line baking dish with greaseproof paper

- Pour in egg, sprinkle with mushrooms and cheddar
- Bake for 5-7 minutes until set
- Heat cream cheese until soft and spread over the top
- Sprinkle onions on top
- Carefully roll up omelette and serve immediately

Lovely served with crusty bread and oven roasted cherry tomatoes.

Toasted Parsnips

3 large firm parsnips, trimmed, peeled and cut into quarters from stem to root.
Salt
50g fresh breadcrumbs
6 tablespoons oil
25g butter

- Pre-heat the oven to 180°C
- Par-boil parsnips in boiling salted water for 4 minutes only
- Drain thoroughly, and then toss in the breadcrumbs, pressing the crumbs on to the parsnips
- Heat the oil and butter together
- When sizzling hot, add parsnips and bake in the pre-heated oven for 1¼ hours
- Turn the parsnips twice during cooking to ensure nice crispy sides all round
- Drain well on kitchen paper.

Wholegrain Rice Salad Niçoise *Serves 6-8*

400g brown long grain rice, cooked, rinsed and drained
1 cucumber, peeled (optional), diced
1 green & 1 red pepper, skinned (optional), diced
6 firm tomatoes, peeled (optional) chopped
125g black olives
2 white onions, chopped
1 clove of garlic, finely chopped
1 small tin of anchovies in oil
135g of tinned drained tuna

Vinaigrette:
4 soupspoons of olive oil
1 soupspoon of vinegar
1 teaspoon of mustard
Salt and pepper to taste.
Or 3 tbsp. of a good vinaigrette dressing.

- Mix all ingredients and leave to rest. Mix well and chill for at least 30 minutes
- Keeps well

Puddings

Athol Brose *Serves 4*

300ml double cream
2 tbsp. clear honey
2-3 tbsp. whisky
50g coarse oatmeal (chopped, toasted almonds can be substituted)

- Whip cream with honey until it forms soft peaks
- Add whisky and whisk until it holds its shape
- Chill in fridge
- Stir in oatmeal before serving

This goes well as an accompaniment with raspberries or blueberries.

Brenda's Chocolate Mousse

225g black chocolate
1 tbsp water
4 eggs

1 tsp, rounded, powdered gelatine
1 small can evaporated milk
1 tbsp. rum or sherry (optional)

- Put chocolate and water in a bowl; dissolve over a pan of gently steaming water
- Remove from heat and cool
- Beat in separated egg yolks
- Dissolve gelatine in water and then add to mixture
- Whisk evaporated milk until stiff and then fold into mixture
- Whisk egg whites until stiff and then fold into mixture with alcohol
- Pour into serving dishes and leave to set.

Grape Clafoutis

800g small white seedless grapes
25g butter
3 egg yolks
1 egg

100g caster sugar
125ml double cream
1 tbsp. flour
Juice of 1 lemon

- Preheat the oven to 200°C
- Wash and dry the grapes
- Butter a large ovenproof 'gratin' style dish and arrange the grapes in the dish as evenly as possible (so they all touch)
- Blend the yolks, egg, sugar, cream and flour in a food processor, add the lemon juice and pour the mixture over the grapes
- Bake in the middle of the oven for about 30 minutes until golden
- Serve slices and eat while warm.

Healthy Fruit Crumble

Stewable fruit, apples, pears, rhubarb etc.
Oatibix, crushed
25g butter per Oatibix

1 tsp brown sugar per Oatibix
Honey to taste
Optional walnuts or almonds, chopped

- Preheat oven to 180°C
- Stew fruit, mix in honey to taste
- Melt butter and mix in Oatibix and sugar
- Spread mixture over stewed fruit and bake for 15-20 minutes.

Hot Trifle *Serves 6 Freezes*

1 Swiss roll
1 can of apricots
2 tbsp. custard powder
2 eggs, separated

1 tbsp. sugar
550ml milk
100g caster sugar
25g blanched almonds

- Pre-heat oven to 180°C
- Slice Swiss roll and arrange with apricots in a 900 ml ovenproof dish
- Blend together custard powder, egg yolks and sugar with a little milk
- Warm rest of milk and make custard
- Pour over Swiss roll and apricots
- Whisk egg whites until stiff and fold in caster sugar
- Pile meringue mixture on top of custard and stud with almonds
- Place in oven for 20 minutes.

Lemon Sussex Pud

1 small cup caster sugar
2 tbsp. plain flour
1 cup milk

1 tbsp. butter
Rind and juice of 1 lemon
2 eggs, separated

- Preheat oven to 180°C
- Beat egg whites
- Cream sugar and butter, blend in plain flour, grated rind and juice of one lemon, mix
- Add cup of milk and 2 well-beaten egg yolks
- Mix thoroughly, fold in 2 stiffly beaten egg whites, and pour into well-greased dish
- Place this into an oven pan of boiling water
- Bake for ½ hour and till golden on top.

Mildred's Rhubarb and Ginger Pudding

675g rhubarb, cut into 3cm pieces
and sugar to taste
225g flour
110g caster sugar
1 tsp. mixed spices
1 tsp. ground ginger

A pinch of salt
110g margarine
1 teacup of milk
1 egg
1 tsp. baking soda, level

- Preheat oven to 160°C
- Place rhubarb into a baking dish, sprinkle with sugar to taste
- Mix margarine, sugar and milk in pan, heat over a gentle heat until margarine is melted
- Add lightly beaten egg and baking soda
- Add this mixture to the dry ingredients and then pour over rhubarb
- Bake for 40-45 minutes or until the top is cooked
- Serve with custard.

Rhubarb and Orange Meringue

450g rhubarb
1 orange
50g granulated sugar

40g cornflour
2 eggs
80g caster sugar

- Preheat oven to 160°C
- Cut up rhubarb and place into an ovenproof dish
- Grate rind and squeeze juice from orange add water to make 350ml of liquid
- Place granulated sugar and cornflour into saucepan, blend in liquid, slowly bring to the boil, and then simmer for 3 minutes
- Allow to cool slightly and then stir egg yolks into orange liquid then pour over rhubarb
- Cook in the centre of oven for 20 minutes
- Turn oven down to 150°C
- Whisk egg whites until stiff then add half caster sugar
- Fold in rest of the sugar and spread mixture over rhubarb
- Cook for another 20 minutes or until browned.

Sara-Jane's Hot Chocolate puddings

250g unsalted butter
125g caster sugar
5 eggs and 5 egg yolks (total 10 Eggs)

250g bitter chocolate (70% + cocoa)
50g plain flour
A few raspberries for decoration

- Whisk 5 egg whites and 10 egg yolks and sugar until you've made a thick sabayon
- In another bowl melt the chocolate and butter together and stir
- When the mixture is off the heat and cooled down a bit, but still smooth and pourable, add it slowly to the sabayon mixture, beating lightly until smooth
  (try not to lose all the air)
- Fold in the sifted flour
- Butter the ramekin moulds and pour mixture into each mould, leave a half centimetre

gap so the mixture can rise in the oven and not spill.
- Then place the ramekins in the fridge for 6 hours
- Preheat oven to 180°C
- Take the ramekins out of the fridge and bake in preheated oven for 10 minutes or until the centres dome and feel dry
- Give the tray a wobble if not sure and if the mixture is still wobbly it probably needs another 2 minutes.

Tipsy Log

1 pack of chocolate chip biscuits
550ml whipping cream

A quantity of sherry or port for dunking
2 tbsp. icing sugar to taste (optional)

- Whip cream and sugar to the stage where it is soft and not too dry
- Pour sherry into small bowl for dunking
- Dunk biscuits, individually, without getting too soggy
- Ice top of biscuit with whipped cream
- Do this for half a dozen biscuits and then put onto their side onto the presentation plate
- From thereon after icing add additional biscuits to the end of the log
- Continue until all biscuits have been used and half of the cream remains
- With the remaining cream ice the log so that all of the biscuits have disappeared
- Ideally put into fridge for 24 hours before eating to allow biscuits to dissolve properly.

Also for an alcohol free version try a Florida Log, substituting orange juice for the sherry If you like alcohol and orange juice then use a mixture of Cointreau and orange juice.

Winter Treacle pudding

100g butter
100g caster sugar
2 large eggs
100g self-raising flour

Grated zest of 1 lemon
$\frac{1}{4}$ tsp. vanilla essence
Pinch of salt
8 large dessert spoons of golden syrup

- Preheat the oven to 180°C
- You'll need four metal pudding moulds and some tin foil
- Butter the pudding moulds well with the spare butter and also a square of foil that's big enough to cover the top of each pudding mould with a 2cm tuck to allow room for each sponge rising.
- Cream the sugar and butter and stir in an egg,
- Add a big spoonful of flour then the other egg
- Stir in the lemon zest and vanilla and the rest of the flour and salt
- Put 2 tbsp. of syrup into each mould
- Divide the sponge mixture into four and spoon into moulds
- Cover with the buttered tin foil not forgetting the pleat to allow space for the pudding to rise
- If you keep the foil tight it steams a bit and is moister
- Cook in the oven for about 35 minutes.

Cakes & Snacks

Apricot and Almond Cake

200g self-raising flour
100g golden sugar
50g dried mixed fruit
25g golden syrup
100g butter

100g finely minced and soaked dry apricots
50g ground almonds
1 lge egg
Almond essence
Milk to mix

- Preheat oven to 170°C
- Rub the fat into the flour and then add the sugar and ground almonds
- Mix in the apricots
- Add fruit, beaten egg, a few drops of almond essence, golden syrup and milk
- Mix to a moist consistency
- Place into a well-greased 23x14cm loaf tin
- Bake for around 1¼ hours or until ready.

To make this more attractive scatter almonds over the top before baking.

Boiled Fruit Cake *Suitable for diabetics*

400g wholemeal self-raising flour
550g mixed fruit including nuts if wanted *
250ml water *
25g Sugar *

100g Butter *
1 level tsp. bicarbonate of soda *
½ tsp. mixed spice
2 eggs, beaten

Optional 1 tbsp port

- Preheat oven to 160°C
- Put all ingredients marked * into a saucepan, bring to the boil then simmer for 3 minutes
- Allow to cool, add remaining ingredients and mix well
- Put into a lined 900g loaf tin
- Bake for 1 hour or until ready.

Cape Brandy Tart

200g stoneless dates, minced or finely chopped
1 level tsp. bicarbonate of soda
135ml boiling water, or half brandy, half water
100g soft butter
200g soft brown sugar
2 eggs, beaten
100g pecan nuts or walnuts, finely chopped

125g self-raising flour
100g glacé cherries, finely chopped

For the syrup
200g soft brown sugar
135ml cold water
135ml cooking brandy

- Preheat oven to 180°C
- Place dates in jug; add the bicarbonate and boiling water
- Cream the butter and sugar in a bowl and gradually add eggs
- Fold in the flour, nuts, and cherries
- Stir in the dates
- Line base of a buttered ovenproof dish or 23cm greased cake tin with Bakewell parchment, then turn mixture into it
- If using loose-bottomed tin, it needs lining with tinfoil
- Place in oven, check after ¾ hour to see if it has been cooked through to the middle
- Bake for 45-60 minutes

Meanwhile, in a saucepan, bring together the syrup ingredients over a low heat, and when the pudding is cooked pour the syrup over it and leave, covered, until cold.

Chocolate Covered Orange Cake

200g flour
200g sugar
220g butter
4 eggs

2 tsp baking powder
230ml freshly squeezed orange juice
Zest of 1 orange
Big bar of milk chocolate

- Preheat oven 180°C,
- Grease 20cm cake pan
- Cream butter and sugar
- Add eggs, one at a time, mixing well after each egg
- Add baking powder, flour and mix
- Add orange juice and zest, mix well
- Pour into pan and bake 45 minutes
- When the cake has cooled, melt the chocolate and pour over cake.
- Leave chocolate to harden (can put in fridge if you don't have much time)

This is a very moist cake so don't worry that the mix is quite wet.

Low-Fat Moist Carrot Cake

Cake:
175g dark brown soft sugar
2 large eggs
120ml sunflower oil
200g wholemeal self-raising flour
1½ level tsp. bicarbonate of soda
3 rounded tsp. mixed spice
Grated zest 1 orange
200g carrots, peeled and grated
175g sultanas

Topping:
250g quark
20g caster sugar
2 tsp. vanilla extract
1 rounded tsp. ground cinnamon and some for dusting

For Syrup Glaze:
Juice ½ small orange
½ tsp. lemon juice
2 tsp. caster sugar

- Preheat oven to 170°C
- Line non-stick oblong tin, 16x25.5cm with parchment paper
- Whisk sugar, eggs and oil in a bowl for 2-3 minutes
- Sift flour, bicarbonate and mixed spices into the bowl and stir
- Fold in orange zest, carrots and sultanas
- Pour mixture into prepared tin and bake in centre of oven for 35-40 minutes, until it is well-risen and feels firm and springy to the touch when lightly pressed in centre.
- Whilst cake is cooling make topping and glaze.

Topping:
Mix all ingredients in bowl until light and fluffy, cover with Clingfilm and chill for 1-2 hours until needed.

Syrup Glaze:
Whisk together juices and sugar in a bowl. When cake comes out stab all over and pour over as evenly as possible. Leave to cool in tin completely. Remove from tin and spread topping over and cut into squares (approx. 12) Dust with cinnamon.

Luscious Lemon Cheesecake

For the Base:
10 digestive biscuits, crushed
55g butter, melted
25g Demerara sugar
For the filling:
150ml double cream
400g can condensed milk

115g low-fat soft cheese, softened
Grated rind and juice of 3 large lemons

For the Topping:
150ml whipping cream, whipped
Fresh strawberries or raspberries to decorate

- Mix together the crushed biscuits, butter and Demerara sugar to make the biscuit base
- Turn into a 20 cm spring-release tin or fluted china flan dish and using a metal spoon, press evenly over the base and sides
- Leave to set
- Mix together the cream, condensed milk, soft cheese and lemon rind, then add the lemon juice a little at a time, whisking until the mixture thickens
- Pour into the flan case and leave covered to chill in the fridge for 3- 4 hours
- Decorate with swirls of whipped cream and fresh fruit.

Polish Apple Cake

140g plain flour
170g golden caster sugar
250ml sunflower oil
4 eggs
1 tsp. baking powder
1 tsp. good quality vanilla essence

Grated zest from 1 lemon
50g freshly made white bread crumbs
5 large cooking apples
2 tsp. ground cinnamon
A little extra golden caster sugar for sprinkling

Checklist:
In addition to the ingredients listed above, you will need: A deep-sided round non-stick cake tin approximately 20 cm in diameter or a deep-sided rectangular Swiss roll tin approximately 20x30 cm in size (better if you want to serve this for dessert).

- Preheat the oven to 180°C
- Brush baking tin with a thin layer of oil
- Apply a thin layer of bread crumbs to the oil in the tin and shake off the excess
- Peel and core 4 apples and cut into thick slices and arrange over the bottom of the tray
- Sprinkle sugar and cinnamon on top of the apples.
- Mix together the flour, sugar, oil, vanilla essence, baking powder, grated lemon and mixed egg mixture, till you get a smooth liquid mixture
- Pour this batter over the apples
- Slice the remaining apple fairly thinly and gently place on top of the batter. It will sink slightly, but that's fine
- Bake in the oven for about 45 minutes, but check after 30 minutes to see how it is doing.

Banana Bread

200g sugar
100g butter, chopped
2 eggs (room temperature)
3 very ripe bananas, chopped (1 extra banana can be added)
1 tsp. baking soda
450g flour
1 tsp. nutmeg
Optional: 100g chocolate chips

- Preheat oven 180°C
- Barely mix the ingredients, cut ripe bananas for added flavour
- Bake in floured and greased bread tin for around 60 minutes

The bread is done when an inserted tester comes out clean and or when the bread begins to separate from the sides. Do not over bake.

Cheesejacks

125g porridge oats
150g cheddar cheese, grated
1 free range egg, beaten
50g butter, melted

½ tsp. rosemary, crushed
1 tsp. rounded, sesame seeds
Salt and pepper to taste
Optional a pinch of paprika

- Preheat the oven to 180°C
- Combine all of the ingredients in a large bowl and mix well
- Press into a 18-20 cm square cake tin and bake for 40 minutes
- Cut into squares

Serve hot or cold.

Easy Choc Chip Cookies

75g margarine
75g brown sugar
1 egg (beaten)
150g self-raising flour

100g choc chips
few drops vanilla essence
pinch of salt

- Preheat oven 180°C
- Cream sugar and margarine
- Beat in egg and essence
- Stir in flour, salt and choc chips
- Roll into balls and flatten, place on greased baking sheet
- Bake 10-15 minutes.

Michael's Flapjacks

110g butter
90g Demerara sugar
90g golden syrup
225g rolled oats
Optional tsp. ground cinnamon, to taste

- Preheat oven to 180°C
- Melt butter, mix in sugar and syrup
- Mix in oats
- Tamp into 20 x 23 cm greased baking tin
- Place in the middle of oven for 25-30 minutes
- leave for 5 minutes to cool before cutting into 3cm squares
- Remove from tin when cool

Hot Apple Brownies

100g self-raising flour
125-150g brown sugar, depending on taste
50g broken walnuts
75g chopped dates

1 tsp. vanilla essence
1 egg
454g unpeeled cooking apples
2 tbsp. melted butter

- Preheat oven to 180°C
- Mix the melted butter, egg, vanilla essence and flour together well
- Mix in sugar, dates and walnuts
- Add cored and chopped but unpeeled apples
- Press into a 23cm round (or 23x15 cm rectangular) greased dish
- Bake for 40 minutes

Serve with cream or hot custard.

Hush Puppies *Makes 30-35*

280g Polenta
70g plain flour, sifted
1 small onion, finely chopped
1 tbsp. caster sugar
2 tbsp. baking powder

½ tsp. salt
175ml milk
1 egg beaten
Corn oil, for deep frying

- Stir dry ingredients together in a bowl and make a well in the centre
- Beat the milk and egg together, then pour into the dry ingredients and stir until a thick batter forms
- Heat at least 5cm of oil in a deep frying pan or saucepan over a high heat, until the temperature reaches 180°C or until a cube of bread browns in 30 seconds.
- Drop in as many teaspoonfuls of the batter as will fit without overcrowding the frying pan and cook, stirring constantly, until the hush puppies puff up and turn golden
- Remove from the oil with a slotted spoon and drain on kitchen paper

Variations can be made by adding cheese or vegetables to the batter before frying.

Oat and Date Slices

150g rolled oats
150g whole-wheat flour
150g butter
50g soft brown sugar

225g dates, stoned and chopped
2 tbsp. water
1 tbsp. lemon juice
1 tbsp. honey

- Preheat oven to 190°C
- Gently simmer dates, water lemon juice and honey until the dates are soft
- Mix oats and flour then rub in fat.
- Stir in sugar
- Place half of the oat mixture in a lined and greased 18 cm square tin, pressing down firmly
- Cover with date mixture
- Place remaining oat mixture on top and press down firmly
- Bake for 30-40 minutes
- Remove from oven and then cut whilst warm
- Remove from tin when cold.

Oat and Raisin Cookies

75g butter, melted and cooled a little
175g Muscovado sugar
200g medium oatmeal
110g wholemeal flour
½ teaspoon bicarbonate of soda

Pinch salt
Pinch cinnamon or mixed spice
75g raisins or more to taste
1 medium egg, beaten

- Preheat oven to 180°C
- Stir beaten egg into melted, cooled butter
- Put rest of ingredients into a large bowl
- Pour in egg and butter mixture and mix to a stiff paste
- Roll mixture into small walnut sized balls
- Space them out well on a greased baking sheet
- Bake for about 10-12 minutes till biscuits feel firm in centre
- Leave to cool on baking sheets
- Ease off with palette knife.

Old Fashioned Ginger Biscuits

110g caster sugar
225g butter
450g plain flour

1 tbsp. ground ginger
1 tsp. baking powder
4 tbsp. golden syrup

- Preheat oven to 180°C
- Beat butter and sugar together
- Add syrup and beat again
- Add half flour, ginger and baking powder, mix well
- Add the remaining flour until mixture holds together, it may not absorb it all
- Roll into small balls and flatten slightly
- Bake on greased tray for 18-20 minutes.

Tiffin

200g rich tea biscuits
200g granulated sugar
200g raisins, sultanas or mixed fruit
1 egg

100g margarine
50g cocoa or chocolate powder
50-100g cooking chocolate

- Melt margarine and sugar in saucepan
- Take off heat add fruit, egg and cocoa and mix well
- Crush all but 4 of the biscuits, add to mixture and stir
- Put into foil lined Swiss roll tin
- Crush remaining biscuits
- When set, pour over melted chocolate and biscuits
- When this has set cut into pieces.

Welsh Griddle Cakes

200g plain flour
½ tsp. baking powder
½ tsp. mixed spice
50g margarine
50g lard

75g currants
50-75g sugar
1 egg
1 tbsp. milk

- Mix and sieve flour baking, powder and mixed spice
- Rub margarine and lard into the flour mixture
- Add rest of the dry ingredients and mix well
- Mix in egg and milk to form a thick paste
- Bake on a griddle/ hot plate over a medium heat until lightly brown on each side

Eat warm or cold, delicious buttered, will store well in an airtight container.

Wheat-Free Chocolate Brownies

125g 72% cocoa chocolate
150g butter or margarine
275g light brown sugar
3 medium eggs
225g 72% cocoa chocolate chips

150g pecans, walnuts and almonds, chopped
1 tsp. vanilla extract
50g rice flour
50g maize flour

- Preheat oven 180°C
- Line a 275mm x175mm tin with non-stick baking paper
- Put chocolate (broken up) and butter in a large bowl and melt, remove from heat
- Stir the sugar into the chocolate and mix well
- Add eggs, one at a time and mix well between each egg. Mixture will start to feel a bit elastic but keep beating
- Add chocolate chips, nuts and vanilla extract and mix well
- Stir in rice flour and maize flour. Pour into tin
- Bake in centre of oven for 40-50 minutes

To check whether brownies are cooked stick a skewer into the centre, it needs to come out slightly sticky. If it comes out clean it is overcooked. Better to undercook, than overcook. Check after 40 minutes, then every 3- 4 minutes thereafter.

Remove brownies from oven and allow to cool substantially while in tin. Remove from tin and place on a cooling rack, cut into squares and allow to cool completely before storing in an airtight container.

Index

Amanda's Slow Cooked lamb	25
Ann's Liver Casserole	28
Apricot and Almond Cake	51
Athol Brose	46
Bacon and Tomato Quiche	39
Banana Bread	55
Beef Carbonnade	10
Beef in Guinness	11
Boiled Fruit Cake (diabetics)	51
Braised Red Cabbage	42
Brenda's Chocolate Mousse	46
Brian's Honeyed Gammon	28
Cape Brandy Tart	52
Carbonara Pasta with Bacon	35
Cheese and Herb Pate	4
Cheese Jacks	55
Cheesy Butternut Pasties	39
Chicken Liver Pate	4
Chicken and Stilton Roulades	16
Chicken Broccoli	16
Chicken Couscous	17
Chicken in Cider	18
Chicken Mornay	19
Chinese Chicken Salad	17
Chocolate Covered Orange Cake	52
Creamy Cider Chicken	18
Curried Parsnip Soup	6
Devilled Chicken	19
Dumplings	12
Easy Choc Chip Cookies	55
Elizabethan Pork	29
Emma's Mozzarella Pasta	35
Exmoor Poachers Pot	25
Fish Soup	6
French Onion Soup	7
Fried Rice	42
German Herring Salad	22
Goulash	12
Grape Clafoutis	46
Healthy Fruit Crumble	47
Hot Apple Brownies	56
Hot Trifle	47
Hunters Pork Chops	29
Hush Puppies (Savoury)	57
Lamb Shanks	26
Leeks and Ham au gratin	30
Leeks in Red Wine	42
Lemon Sussex Pud	47
Liver Bonne Femme	26
Low-Fat Moist Carrot Cake	53
Luscious Lemon Cheesecake	53
Macaroni Cheese and Tuna	36
Michael's Flapjacks	56
Mildred's Rhubarb and Ginger Pudding	48
Mushroom, Egg and Cheese Tartlets	40
Mushroom Polonaise	43
New Orleans Prawns	23
Oat and Date Slices	57
Oat and Raisin Cookies	58
Old Fashioned Ginger Biscuits	58
Onion Soup	7
Onion Tart	40
Paprika Pork	30
Pasta with Parma Ham	36
Pasta Surprise	37
Pheasant Pate	5
Polish Apple Cake	54
Pork and Ginger Casserole	31
Pork Parcels	31
Prawn Stir Fry	23
Rhubarb and Orange Meringue	48
Risotto	43
Roasted Red Pepper Soup	7
Roasted Red Pepper, Sweet Potato & Onion Soup	8
Rolled Mushroom Omelette	43
Sam's Sausage Hotpot	32
Sara-Jane's Hot Chocolate Puddings	48
Sausage Meat Plait with Baked Apple	32
Savoury Sausage Roly Poly	33
Smoked Trout Pate	5
Spicy Spare Rib Chops	33
Steak and Kidney Pie	12
Steph's Salmon Parcel	22
Tiffin	58
Tipsy Log	49
Toasted Parsnips	44
Tomato and Orange Soup	8
Trout with Almonds and Dill	22
Turkey Pate	5
Venison Casserole	13
Warming Beef Stew	14
Waterzooi Gantoise	20
Welsh Griddle Cakes	59
Wheat-Free Chocolate Brownies	59
Wholegrain Rice Salad Nicoise	44
Winter Treacle Pudding	49